Youtube For Beginners:

Learn The Basics of Youtube, Get More Views, Likes, Attract New Subscribers, Earn Money Secrets Guide

By

Joseph Joyner

Table of Contents

Introduction 5

Chapter 1. Create Unique Content Frequently 6

Chapter 2. Building a Great YouTube Video Title 8

Chapter 3. Tagging Your Videos Properly 12

Chapter 4. Description Is Key 13

Chapter 5. Tips on How to Get More Views 14

Chapter 6. How to Get More Subscribers for Your YouTube Channel 17

Chapter 7. What Kind of Money Can You Make From YouTube? 23

Chapter 8. Final Words 27

Thank You Page 29

Youtube For Beginners: Learn The Basics of Youtube, Get More Views, Likes, Attract New Subscribers, Earn Money Secrets Guide

By Joseph Joyner

Introduction

There are several reasons why you might decide to start up a YouTube channel, but regardless of your reason for starting your channel the desired outcome is the same. You want to create content regularly and frequently, that is high quality and unique and works to build a brand for yourself so that you're able to gain more views and more subscribers. At the end of the day the goal is to get your videos in front of as many eyeballs as possible so that you can get your message, cause, product, service or company out there.

Chapter 1. Create Unique Content Frequently

The most popular YouTubers generate a lot of content and generally create some sort of hook. Think of what keeps people coming back to traditional TV outlets, generally speaking they'll see an episode of a show and they'll enjoy it, so they'll come back the next time it's on. This is why it's important for you to generate scheduled content and not leave your subscribers hanging.

It really depends on what you're planning on doing. If you're building a channel that is based around current events and news and you're the only presenter then the most important thing will be the consistency of your videos. If you say that you're going to put out videos once a day do it, if you say that you're going to put out videos on Mondays, Wednesdays and Fridays, make sure you do it.

If you can come up with an idea that generates a viral response you're going to gain tonnes of natural views and subscribers. Get your viewers involved in your video creation process, meaning maybe you can ask them to do something for your videos, people love being involved. You can utilize things like Twitter hashtags for this or even create a Facebook fan page for your YouTube channel and community. People love to belong and creating a community based around your idea where people generate natural discussions without you having to do anything, will raise your exposure.

If you have to choose to sacrifice video quality in favour of video frequency you should do it. This is because the majority of people are willing to forgive some video quality in favour of getting to hear what you have to say. It really depends on what your channel is about. To go with the same example if you're doing a current events and news channel then the quality of how you look doesn't necessarily have to be 60fps 1080p. People are going to be fine with 720p or sometimes even less, in favour of getting your content frequently. This becomes very important when you're doing current events because well, you want your video commentary to be current for said current events.

Chapter 2. Building a Great YouTube Video Title

Search Engine Optimization is key for all aspects of online marketing. This term might be scary for those who are just starting out, but it's really simple. SEO is simply understanding how a specific search engine figures out who should come up first, second, third etc. when certain keywords are plugged into the search engine. This is no different for YouTube, obviously if you could you would want your videos to always come up first right? More views, more subscribers. How often do you go to page 12 and start looking for videos?

The titles of your YouTube videos are an extremely important part of making sure that your videos appear high in the list. You need to do some market research and figure out what people are actually searching for. If you accidentally use some language in your title that is uncommon or infrequent and you don't already have a tonne of subscribers, then many people won't have the opportunity to even view your video and pass judgment on its quality.

You can produce an amazing video, but if people aren't able to find it, it isn't going to have a chance of going viral. Due to how YouTube's SEO algorithm works, the title is actually very important because the title of your video actually becomes the <title></title> on the video's landing page.

The specific language you choose to use is tremendously important with your title. You're going to know what your video is about, but if you don't explain the video quickly in a way that most other people are going to think of when they search, then you're going to lose a lot of views. Search Google for free keyword research tools and figure out what people are searching for that is relevant to your niche. If you're getting into giving workout advice and your video is you giving workout tips around lifting weights, you'll need to know how people will search for that. Do they say "lifting advice" or do they say "weightlifting"

When you use keyword research programs you can essentially type in a search that you would do if you were looking for your video and if your language can be improved the program will suggest similar words to help boost your SEO. Handy right?

Other Things to Consider When Creating a YouTube Video Title

Take your time and be smart. The title is extremely important and while you might think you've done so much amazing work with your video, if you don't optimize your video through things like the title and the tags then you're going to be in a world of hurt. You don't want all of your hard work to go to waste.

It seems like it's pretty obvious, but try to explain you video with a little bit more detail. If you don't explain the video and instead just put something like WOWWWWW!!!!!! people are not going to be able to find it. It could be the best video uploaded on YouTube, but if you aren't descriptive, yet concise people aren't going to find it. I can't reiterate this fact enough, you might be super excited about the video that you've taken or created, but take a little time and think of a witty descriptive title.

Study your competition. Remember that you've got competition on YouTube. Unless you're creating some magnificent new genre of video, you're going to be competing with already established YouTubers that have been at it for a long time. If you're in the weight loss and fitness niche you might want to search other users in that field and see how they title, tag and describe their videos. See how often they post and try to get ideas from them. You'll want to make sure that you come up with something unique or make sure that your style isn't precisely the same as them or you might be seen as a copycat or fraud, but it is important to understand other people who have come before you and see which of their videos have been most successful by view count and which have been the least successful.

Chapter 3. Tagging Your Videos Properly

When it comes to tagging your videos there are a few things you should do. First learn to start broad so that you grab all possible viewers. If you're doing Comedy make sure you use that tag. Use any brand specific tags that you've come up with. Make sure to look at your competitors videos and see the tags that they use. Make sure you use tags that are a little more specific as well. Use YouTube's auto tagging tools because these tools have become very good, don't get too fancy.

Chapter 4. Description Is Key

You want to be as descriptive as possible with your videos, without being obscure. Advertisement SEO tools will help you with this process and will suggest synonyms for you, but at the same you don't want to be under describing something. Instead of naming your video "Awesome Dogs!" You could say "Awesome Dogs, Doing Awesome Tricks" if tricks is what those dogs were doing. Add as much description as possible, this can't be overstated.

Chapter 5. Tips on How to Get More Views

If you've watched plenty of successful YouTubers you will quickly pick up on the marketing strategies that they utilize to get more attention. They will try to create viral trends on other platforms such as Twitter by asking their users to tweet things with a specific hashtag for their next video. This is an example of a way that you can pull more people to your videos. Your YouTube video comment section is a very closed off place to have a discussion, if you have your users take it to Twitter there is a chance that your hashtag will get shared with someone popular, who in turn might retweet it to their followers. If this happens you can generate more attention that will send people back to YouTube generating a lot more views for you. Again, the idea is to get as many eyeballs as possible seeing your brand, your name, your channel and your video.

Use annotations on your videos, but don't overdo it. An annotation is a pop up on the video that a user can click on as a call to action. You can make annotations for viewers to subscribe to your channel or to thumbs up your video if they've liked it. Another thing that is very useful to get more views across your channel is if you've made related videos or you're going to reference an old video in your new video you can create an annotation linking the viewer back to the old video, which will in turn video you views on both videos.

Don't overdo your annotations, some channels (generally unsuccessful ones) will go nuts with annotations and they will fill the video screen with them trying to essentially force someone into committing an error and making them click on the annotation. This is a nuisance and will piss of viewers, so don't do it!

Utilize Playlists to Get more Views

There are a lot of reasons why using playlists can get you more views. Naturally if you have a series of videos on one subject and you put them in order on a playlist people are more likely to stick around and not wander off to watch another channel, especially if your content is solid.

Another thing you can benefit from is if someone walks away from the computer sometimes they will leave a playlist running which will give you extra views. This isn't a bad tactic on your part and isn't your fault, but I would simply make sure that your content was solid and that you only group things together that make sense to be in a playlist.

The number one way to get more channel views, is to get more subscribers! Let's face it these other methods are a way to get more views and hopefully get more subscribers, but really if you have a good subscriber base then people will be waiting for you to release videos, so this essentially a guaranteed view each time you release a video.

Chapter 6. How to Get More Subscribers for Your YouTube Channel

Many of the strategies for gaining subscribers are the same as the strategies for gaining views. Why? Because a subscriber is just a satisfied viewer that is excited to see more content from you. Subscribers and Viewers actually act as a conduit for each other, if you consider the fact that every subscriber is going to likely view your videos and that views are likely to get you more subscribers.

The number one thing you need to do is post useful content on a regular basis. As I said before unless the quality of your videos is key to the niche you're involved in if you want to save some time on uploading and rendering you can feel free to reduce the quality a bit to meet your frequency needs, just make sure the content is unique and useful for the viewer and potential subscriber.

Just as with getting more viewers ensure that you title your videos with best SEO practices in mind and be as descriptive as possible, remember getting more viewers will get you more subscribers and getting more subscribers will get you more views.

Another important way you're going to get more subscribers is by putting effort into your channel itself and your social media presence. If users decide they might want to subscribe to your channel, they're first likely going to go to your channel and view several of your videos, if they show up there and the content is solid they're likely to subscribe, but another important thing to keep in mind is your channel design.

You need to make sure your channel header/banner and thumbnail icon are very good. Keep in mind that the thumbnail icon is very small and should not be too complex. If your channel art is well done you're likely to benefit from that. There are lots of places you can make great graphics even if you have no graphical design skill, just do a Google search. If you really want something good, you can consider hiring a freelance designer to create some content for you, it won't cost you too much and you will likely get a return on your investment if you're serious about your video creation.

Show Your Viewers That You're Human

An important method for gaining subscribers is to just be yourself and show your viewers that you are indeed a flesh and blood human being. The genre and niche of your videos is really important to figuring out how to do this. If you're already doing comedy then showing your lighter side isn't really going to be all that relevant, but if you take on serious topics often than showing people your lighter side can be really useful for getting subscribers. If people feel like they know you, they'll follow you to hell and back.

Another reason to keep your content fresh and show your lighter side is because you want to keep viewers and subscribers on their toes, you don't want people to get bored with your content so when you get into the groove of things, throw a monkey wrench in there every once and awhile.

Consider shooting your videos with various backdrops or in different locations. Switch things up every little bit. Utilization of a green screen will give you the ability to change things up very easily and make it look as though you're anywhere.

Simply Ask People to Subscribe

If you're the kind of hard working person that I think you are, you've likely started doing most of the things in this tutorial/guide. You're doing your best and you're grinding it out, but maybe you're afraid to just ask people to subscribe to you because you're far too humble.

People are generally nice and yes even on the internet they can be. If you've got great content, don't be afraid to just ask people if they wouldn't mind subscribing. You can also offer them something if they do subscribe, but you need to be able to make sure you can deliver. Don't false advertise! If you tell viewers that once you get X amount of subscribers you'll start doing an extra video a week, you better be ready and able to get that done otherwise your subscribers might lose respect for you.

Know When to Act and When to Be Yourself

This is probably one of the most underappreciated aspects to being a great content creator online. Too many people try to be someone else, but viewers can tell when you're not being genuine. There is a time for acting and there is a time when you should just relax and be yourself. Of course it might be tempted to act if you want to be super funny and attract people in that manner, but using the example of making a channel based around current events and news, sometimes just being relaxed and just being personally passionate is the best medicine for your YouTube channel.

Talk to people the way you would if they were with you in your house. Talk to people like you would your friends. A lot of the time people think they'll get into producing content online because people they know say, "You really know a lot about this topic, have you considered making YouTube videos?" and you said, "Yeah that would be a great idea." But then when you get to it, you start trying to be somebody else. Just be yourself and the people on YouTube will view you in the same light.

Make Use of a Trailer Video

When a potential subscriber lands on your channel they're going to be met with a trailer if you've created one. This is a great opportunity to create a video that highlights what your channel is about and to ask people to subscribe to your channel. This is where your marketing skills need to shine because in just a minute to a minute and a half you should be able to sell yourself. Tell potential subscribers why they should subscribe and what they should expect to get out of you if they become a subscriber.

Create Video Responses to Popular Videos

This is a great way for you to shine. This works best when you're dealing with hot topic current event style news. If someone posts an opinion video and you want to counter them in a hot debate you might be able to draw views from their viewers. It's important to note that if you're disagreeing with a very popular narrative or with someone who is very popular it might generate notoriety and animosity from their subscribers, but this will get you views. You might also be able to pull in subscriptions from those who agree with you.

Chapter 7. What Kind of Money Can You Make From YouTube?

It's become the new dream job. Quit your day job and become a full time YouTuber and become YouTube famous! Who wouldn't love to make a living spouting off about whatever they would love? Making money from YouTube really depends on what you're making videos for. Making money from YouTube itself is harder than it looks. The latest figures available show that Google pays $7.62 per 1000 ad views. You have to also consider that this is gross revenue and doesn't include business expenses. If you're going to make really good YouTube videos you're going to have to spend a lot of money on video editing. You can make a living, but you're going to have to be quite successful, don't expect to earn a living from YouTube when you're just starting up.

If you're doing YouTube videos as a marketing strategy for a company, then it's a whole different ballgame. If you can create a strong call to action to purchase whatever it is that you're selling then your expenditures on marketing through YouTube can be very minimal in comparison to the return you'll get through extra sales, especially if you create a viral trend.

If you are doing YouTube videos as a solo artist don't despair, there are other ways to generate revenue.

Create a Store For your Channel

You can turn your YouTube brand into a store. Create a gift shop of sorts, sell shirts and other trinkets. Consider writing an eBook to sell to your subscribers. If you can turn your YouTube channel into a business you will be able to benefit in the same way another company could.

Create a Patreon Account

Patreon is website where freelance artists including YouTube video creators can go and ask for assistance in crowdfunding their content. If you can get enough subscribers that want to see you make more videos, more often and with better quality then you might be able to generate enough money monthly through donations to be able to move to making videos full time. Patreon is an amazing way for you to make the jump from part time to full time YouTuber.

Sign Your Own Sponsors

If you can sign a sponsor then you can get more money for views based on a contract that you make with the sponsor yourself. This means you'll be cutting out the middle-man and making money directly. Sponsors will have to approve of your content and believe honestly that a sponsorship deal with you is going to create a return on their investment. Nobody gives money away without the hopes of it being a positive investment, so you'll have to make it worth their while.

Create Premium Content

Build content for free on YouTube and then create a call to action to draw subscribers and viewers to your website and have them purchase premium content from you. You'll have to be able to have the time to generate premium content and the content will have to be worth the cost. A lot of popular news-type YouTube outlets have websites and premium content. This happens a lot with political oriented channels, such as The Young Turks or PJ Media.

You can choose to charge people per episode or ask for a monthly fee. If you set a monthly fee at just $8 and you only need to get 200 steady premium clients to make $2,800 a month. Premium content is the motherload, but it will require you to make very solid videos. People pay only $8 now for a monthly subscription to Netflix so you'll have to make your decisions wisely. You could choose to lower the price and draw in more possible premium clients and possibly make more money, but you'll have to do an analysis on these numbers.

Chapter 8. Final Words

Let's sum it all up. If you want to be a successful YouTuber you're going to need to create frequent content that people enjoy. You'll have to satisfy a niche in the market and over time create better quality videos. You'll need to be sure to tag your videos properly and make sure that you come up with awesome and descriptive titles for your videos.

You'll need to create a social media presence to engage with subscribers even more and get your videos in front of even more people. You'll need to generate solid channel artwork that makes you look like you really give a damn about the work you do. You'll have to learn to be natural in front of the camera. All of these things will help to generate more views and more subscribers. Just be genuine with your viewers and they will respect you for it.

If you want to be able to create the best videos possible you are going to need to generate revenue so that you can buy the best equipment. Sell your own merchandise, Partner with YouTube so that you can get ad revenue, Sign up for Patreon so that happy subscribers can give you money per video or monthly. Try to find sponsorships that can help you get some great equipment and create even better videos.

At the end of the day these are all the things that you need to do to improve your YouTube presence. The most important rule of all is that you need to not give up. Don't expect instant success, don't expect people to fall for your charm overnight. Expect many bumps in the road, but expect that with practice you will get better. Expect with hard work you will eventually be successful. Listen to your subscribers because at the end of the day they are your customers and in the end the customer is always right.

If you want to be successful on YouTube emulate those who have been successful before you and find a way to provide unique content in your specific niche. Fill a demand that isn't being filled. Consider reading comments on your competitors videos and see what people are asking for, if those YouTubers aren't already servicing the needs of their subscribers, then you can do it for them.

Thank You Page

I want to personally thank you for reading my book. I hope you found information in this book useful and I would be very grateful if you could leave your honest review about this book. I certainly want to thank you in advance for doing this.

If you have the time, you can check my other books too.

www.ingramcontent.com/pod-product-compliance
Lightning Source LLC
Chambersburg PA
CBHW071554080326
40690CB00056B/2039